ENDANGERED AND THREATENED ANIMALS

THE TIGER

A MyReportLinks.com Book

Carl R. Green

MyReportLinks.com Books
an imprint of
Enslow Publishers, Inc. E
Box 398, 40 Industrial Road
Berkeley Heights, NJ 07922
USA

MyReportLinks.com Books, an imprint of Enslow Publishers, Inc. MyReportLinks is a trademark of Enslow Publishers, Inc.

Library of Congress Cataloging-in-Publication Data

Green, Carl R.
  The tiger / Carl R. Green.
     p. cm. — (Endangered and threatened animals)
Summary: Discusses what tigers are, why they are endangered, what their current status is, and what is being done to help them. Includes Internet links to Web sites related to tigers.
Includes bibliographical references (p.   ) and index.
  ISBN 0-7660-5059-9
  1. Tigers—Juvenile literature. 2. Endangered species—Juvenile literature. [1. Tigers. 2. Endangered species.] I. Title. II. Series.
QL737.C23G7254 2003
599.756—dc21

                          2002014862

Printed in the United States of America

10 9 8 7 6 5 4 3 2 1

To Our Readers:
Through the purchase of this book, you and your library gain access to the Report Links that specifically back up this book.
The Publisher will provide access to the Report Links that back up this book and will keep these Report Links up to date on **www.myreportlinks.com** for three years from the book's first publication date.
We have done our best to make sure all Internet addresses in this book were active and appropriate when we went to press. However, the author and the Publisher have no control over, and assume no liability for, the material available on those Internet sites or on other Web sites they may link to.
The usage of the MyReportLinks.com Books Web site is subject to the terms and conditions stated on the Usage Policy Statement on **www.myreportlinks.com**.
In the future, a password may be required to access the Report Links that back up this book. The password is found on the bottom of page 4 of this book.
Any comments or suggestions can be sent by e-mail to comments@myreportlinks.com or to the address on the back cover.

Photo Credits: Convention of International Trade in Endangered Species of Wild Fauna and Flora, p. 24; © Corel Corporation, pp. 1, 3, 10, 11, 12, 15, 18, 20, 30; Defenders of Wildlife, p. 28; Digital Vision, pp. 16, 34, 35; Forever Tigers, p. 22; Global Tiger Patrol, p. 27; International Year of the Tiger Foundation, p. 32; John Bavaro, p. 17; MyReportLinks.com Books, p. 4; Shambala Preserve, p. 38; The Tiger Information Center, p. 37; University of Michigan Museum of Zoology, p. 40; WWF Global Network, p. 14.

Cover Photo: Digital Vision

Contents

MyReportLinks.com Books
Great Books, Great Links, Great for Research!

MyReportLinks.com Books present the information you need to learn about your report subject. In addition, they show you where to go on the Internet for more information. The pre-evaluated Report Links that back up this book are kept up to date on **www.myreportlinks.com**. With the purchase of a MyReportLinks.com Books title, you and your library gain access to the Report Links that specifically back up that book. The Report Links save hours of research time and link to dozens—even hundreds—of Web sites, source documents, and photos related to your report topic.

Please see "To Our Readers" on the Copyright page for important information about this book, the MyReportLinks.com Books Web site, and the Report Links that back up this book.

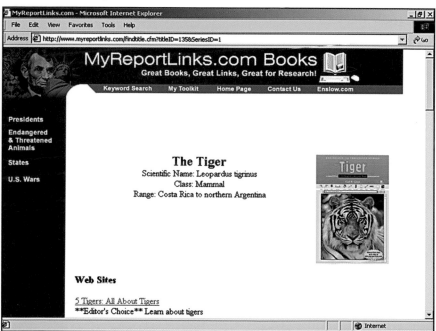

Access:

The Publisher will provide access to the Report Links that back up this book and will try to keep these Report Links up to date on our Web site for three years from the book's first publication date. Please enter **ETG7746** if asked for a password.

Report Links

The Internet sites described below can be accessed at
http://www.myreportlinks.com

EDITOR'S CHOICE

▶ 5 Tigers: All About Tigers

At this Web site you will learn about the evolution of tigers, where they
live, and how many there are. You will also learn about their behavior
and physical characteristics.

Link to this Internet site from http://www.myreportlinks.com

EDITOR'S CHOICE

▶ Endangered Species: Tiger

At the World Wildlife Fund Web site you will find a detailed article
about tigers exploring their habitat, hunting techniques, mating rituals,
and threats. You will also find descriptions of areas where tigers live
such as Bhutan, Indochina, and Russia.

Link to this Internet site from http://www.myreportlinks.com

EDITOR'S CHOICE

▶ Kids Planet

Kids Planet provides information about endangered species around the
world. You will also find information about the Endangered Species
Act and learn how a species gets listed as endangered.

Link to this Internet site from http://www.myreportlinks.com

EDITOR'S CHOICE

▶ Tigers in the Wild: Wanted Alive

Here you will find a brief history of tigers, their cultural significance,
and evolution. Learn about threats facing the tiger, their current global
distribution, and efforts being made to protect the tiger by the World
Wildlife Federation.

Link to this Internet site from http://www.myreportlinks.com

EDITOR'S CHOICE

▶ Kids for Tigers

This Web site provides information about saving tigers and news
related to tigers. You can also visit "The Tiger's Den" to learn about
the evolution, behavior, family life, and history of the tiger.

Link to this Internet site from http://www.myreportlinks.com

EDITOR'S CHOICE

▶ Cybertiger

At the National Geographic Web site for kids you can become the
virtual zookeeper of a Cyber Tiger. Articles about tigers from *National
Geographic* magazine are also provided.

Link to this Internet site from http://www.myreportlinks.com

The Internet sites described below can be accessed at
http://www.myreportlinks.com

All for Tigers!
Here you will find brief fact sheets on the Bengal, Indochinese, Siberian, South China, and Sumatran tigers. You will also find fact sheets on the Bali, Caspian, and Javan, which are now extinct.

Link to this Internet site from http://www.myreportlinks.com

Awesome Tigers
Did you know that three subspecies of the tiger are already extinct? At this Web site you will find profiles on both living and extinct tiger subspecies. An image gallery and a question and answer section are also provided.

Link to this Internet site from http://www.myreportlinks.com

Bengal Tiger
This Web site provides a profile on the Bengal tiger, where you can find out about its habitat, diet, and threats.

Link to this Internet site from http://www.myreportlinks.com

Bengal Tiger: American Museum of Natural History
At this Web site you will find a brief profile of the Bengal tiger, where you will learn about its diminished population and about questions regarding reintroduction of the tiger into China.

Link to this Internet site from http://www.myreportlinks.com

Bengal Tigers
This Web site provides a collection of images of large cats, including Bengal and White tigers.

Link to this Internet site from http://www.myreportlinks.com

CITES
The Convention on International Trade in Endangered Species of Wild Fauna and Flora Web site describes what CITES is, how it works, and CITES species. You will also find a list of participating countries.

Link to this Internet site from http://www.myreportlinks.com

Report Links

 The Internet sites described below can be accessed at
http://www.myreportlinks.com

▶ Endangered Species

EE Link Endangered Species Web site provides links to species facts, endangered species lists, laws and policy, and educational resources for kids. You can also read current news and learn how to take action.

Link to this Internet site from http://www.myreportlinks.com

▶ Endangered Species: Tiger

At this Web site you will find a brief summary of the tiger situation, including the number of tigers remaining. You will also learn about threats facing the species. Click on "Tigers in Detail" for more information.

Link to this Internet site from http://www.myreportlinks.com

▶ The Endangered Species Program

At the U.S. Fish & Wildlife Web site you will learn about their Endangered Species Program. Information about species, laws and polices, and a kids section are available.

Link to this Internet site from http://www.myreportlinks.com

▶ Forever Tigers

Forever Tigers explores the threats facing the tiger. It contains articles about tigers, a gallery of images, and an interactive map revealing the diminished population of the tiger over the years.

Link to this Internet site from http://www.myreportlinks.com

▶ Global Tiger Patrol

Global Tiger Patrol is a global organization working to educate the public and help in the effort to save the tiger from extinction. Information about tigers, the tiger crisis, and the organization's conservation projects are examined.

Link to this Internet site from http://www.myreportlinks.com

▶ International Year of the Tiger Foundation

International Year of the Tiger Foundation is working to prevent the extinction of the wild tiger. The organization's site includes narrative about the plight of the tiger, as well as information about the worldwide distribution of the remaining tiger population.

Link to this Internet site from http://www.myreportlinks.com

 The Internet sites described below can be accessed at
http://www.myreportlinks.com

Panthera Tigris: Tiger

The Animal Diversity Web site presents scientific data about the tiger.
Here you will learn the scientific classification, geographic range, physical
characteristics, and natural history of the species.

Link to this Internet site from http://www.myreportlinks.com

The Roar Foundation: Shambala Preserve

At this Web site you can make an online visit to the Shambala Preserve,
located forty miles northeast of Los Angeles, California, near the Mojave
Desert. The Shambala Preserve holds seventy animals, including Siberian and
Bengal tigers.

Link to this Internet site from http://www.myreportlinks.com

Save China's Tigers

At this Web site you will find information about the role of the tiger in
Chinese culture, its status in China today, and news items about preservation
and conservation efforts.

Link to this Internet site from http://www.myreportlinks.com

Sumatran Tiger

This site has a fact sheet on the Sumatran tiger where you will learn about its
classification, diet, habitat, life span, range, and other facts.

Link to this Internet site from http://www.myreportlinks.com

TigerAid Foundation

The TigerAid Foundation is committed to generating awareness of the
plight of the tiger. Information about ongoing threats, a description of the
foundation, and a gallery of pictures are found here.

Link to this Internet site from http://www.myreportlinks.com

Tigers in Crisis

Tigers in Crisis presents a discussion of the problems tigers face in the wild
and possible solutions. You will also find extensive information about the
Bengal, Siberian, and Sumatran tigers.

Link to this Internet site from http://www.myreportlinks.com

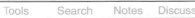
Report Links

The Internet sites described below can be accessed at
http://www.myreportlinks.com

▶ **The Tiger Foundation**
This Web site offers a wealth of information about tigers, including
facts about tigers, their ecology, issues facing these animals, and
overviews of all eight tiger subspecies.

Link to this Internet site from http://www.myreportlinks.com

▶ **Tigers at the Gate**
This *Smithsonian Magazine* article about tigers presents a brief
historical overview of the relationship between humans and tigers.
You will also find links to other related Smithsonian articles.

Link to this Internet site from http://www.myreportlinks.com

▶ **Tiger Island**
Tiger Island is an interactive tiger exhibit at Dreamworld, a theme park
located in Australia. The site provides a narrative about the exhibit, as
well as facts, trivia, and photographs of tigers. You will also find
information concerning existing threats to tigers in the wild.

Link to this Internet site from http://www.myreportlinks.com

▶ **The Tiger's Paw**
The Tiger's Paw Web site presents a collection of information and
resources about tigers, their plight, and ongoing conservation efforts.
There is also a discussion forum.

Link to this Internet site from http://www.myreportlinks.com

▶ **Tiger Time**
Tiger Time is an interactive online adventure developed by *National
Geographic*. The adventure tells the story of a *National Geographic*
photographer whose assignment was to study tigers in India.

Link to this Internet site from http://www.myreportlinks.com

▶ **Wild Cat Species and Distribution—Asia**
Big Cats Online provides a description of the five tiger subspecies
across the continent of Asia and where they are located. Additional
tools include key facts, photographs, and additional links.

Link to this Internet site from http://www.myreportlinks.com

Scientific Name

Panthera tigris. Historically, there are eight subspecies.

Endangered Subspecies (5)

Bengal (Indian), Chinese, Indochinese, Siberian, and Sumatran tigers.

Extinct Subspecies (3)

Caspian, Bali, and Javan tigers.

Lifespan

In the wild, twelve to fifteen years; in captivity, twenty years or longer.

Size* (Bengal Tiger)

Adult Male:
Length: 106–122 in.
(269.24–309.88 cm.)
Height: 36–44 in.
(91.44–111.76 cm.)
Weight: 385–570 lbs.
(174.63–258.55 kg.)

Adult Female:
Length: 97–105 in.
(246.38–266.7 cm.)
Height: 36–44 in.
(91.44–111.76 cm.)
Weight: 220–385 lbs.
(99.79–174.63 kg.)

Pelage (Coat of Fur)

Orange-gold, black striped coat with white underbelly. White, black striped tigers are rare in the wild.

*Figures represent average measurements.

Gestation Period

93 to 111 days

Number of Young

Litters of two to seven cubs.

Diet

Hoofed mammals, such as deer and wild pigs.

Territory (Range)

Male Bengal tigers rule a territory of some 40-square miles (64.37 sq. km.). Females occupy smaller ranges within the male's territory.

Threats to Survival

Loss of habitat and poaching.

Current Habitat

Largest populations inhabit the forests of Southeast Asia. Smaller populations survive in the cedar forests of Northern Asia and on the island of Sumatra.

Current Population*

Today's wild tiger population ranges from between 5,000 to 7,000. Subspecies numbers range from 3,000 Bengal tigers to as few as 400 Siberian tigers and fewer than 100 Chinese tigers.

Legislative Status

Most surviving tigers live in parks and reserves, protected by endangered species laws.

Panthera tigris

A Bengal tiger slips silently through the heavy brush. The slanting rays of the setting sun seem to strike golden sparks from its tawny coat. In a nearby clearing, swamp deer look up, startled. The great predator stops, every sense alert. Its black-striped body blends into the high grass. The deer toss their heads, snort, and return to their feeding.

Noiseless on padded feet, the tiger slips closer to its prey. All at once the deer catch the tiger's scent. As they turn to run, the tiger springs into the clearing. One of the does stumbles and goes down on her knees. With two mighty bounds, the tiger is on her. Razor-sharp claws rip at the doe's flanks as powerful jaws close on her throat. Her

▲ Bengal tigers, native to India, are like other subspecies of tigers in that they are keen hunters.

windpipe crushed, the doe collapses and dies. The tiger quickly drags the carcass into the underbrush. Like most cats, the hunter keeps its kill to itself.

▶ A Family of Fierce Predators

Watch a house cat as it stalks a mouse. Except for size and color, the cat could well be a Bengal tiger stalking a swamp deer. This fact does not surprise scientists who study the cat family. All cats, from house pets to lions and tigers, belong to the family *Felidae*. House cats (*Felis catus*) and tigers (*Panthera tigris*), however, are on separate branches of the family tree.

Despite some similarities, tigers are not closely related to the long-extinct saber-toothed tiger (*Smilodon fatalis*).

▲ Leopards, like the one above, are close cousins to tigers. The same is true for lions and jaguars.

The tiger's closest cousins in the genus *Panthera* are lions, leopards, and jaguars. All four species can be traced to a long-ago ancestor the *Proailurus Lemanensis*. The fossil record shows that tigers have been around for some two million years.[1]

In captivity, tigers and lions can—and do—interbreed. A female tiger that mates with a lion produces cubs called *ligers*. If the father is a tiger and the mother a lion, the cubs are called *tigons*. Like the mule, these crossbreeds cannot produce offspring. In California's Shambala Preserve, however, a tigon named Noelle once surprised the experts. The tigon gave birth to a cub sired by a male tiger. Actress Tippy Hedren, the preserve's founder, says that Noelle "spoke" both *lion* and *tiger*—but spoke only *tiger* to her ti-tigon cub.[2]

▶ A Creature of Legend

Over the years the tiger has been both admired and feared. In the 1700s, an Indian sultan's royal banner proclaimed, "The Tiger Is God."[3] Shiva, the Hindu god of salvation as well as of destruction, is often drawn with a tiger's face. "Every creature in the jungle trembled when it sensed my approach," observed the proud tiger of R. K. Narayan's novel, *A Tiger for Malgudi*. "Let them tremble and understand who is the master . . . of this world."[4]

Folktales, though, tend to describe the tiger in less awesome terms. One such tale, told in Thailand, explains how the tiger got its stripes. Long ago, when all tigers were a solid orange-gold in color, there came a time of heavy rains. During a break in the downpour, a hungry tiger pounced on an old woodcutter.

The old man thought fast. "A great flood is coming!" he cried. "To save ourselves, we must build a bamboo raft." The slow-thinking tiger agreed, and the two went to work. When they were done, the old man pointed to the sky. "The rains are coming," he cried. "I better tie you to the raft so you can't fall off."

The tiger did as it was told. After roping the great beast to the raft, the old man fled. When at last the tiger realized that it had been tricked, it took the animal a full day to break free. As each rope broke, it left a ragged black scar on

WWF Tigers in the Wild - History and Culture - Microsoft Internet Explorer

File   Edit   View   Favorites   Tools   Help

Address   http://www.panda.org/resources/publications/species/tiger99/history_and_culture.html

WWF

- Executive Summary
- The Tiger in History and Culture
  - Evolution of the Tiger
  - Eight Subspecies of Tigers
- WWF's Campaign for Tiger Conservation
- The Threats Facing the Tiger
- The Tiger at a Glance
- What WWF Is Doing
- The Tiger of the Year
- What Needs to be Done

Tigers in the wild

The tiger has always been a muse, a creature of awe, embodied in culture and religion. The earliest evidence comes from 5,000 years ago, sculpted on seals of the Indus Valley civilization of Harappa and Mohenjo-Daro, now in Pakistan. Frequent references to tigers appear in the Mahabharata and the Ramayana, the epic poems of the Aryan peoples who entered India from the northwest 4,000 years ago. The tiger appears as a symbol of beauty, power, and ferocity. Hinduism's female deity, Durga, is depicted riding on a tiger. Her image is widely displayed and can often be seen painted on the sides of trucks.

A Chinese girl wears a tiger hat hoping she will become as powerful and robust as the animal. PETER JACKSON

In China, people interpreted the markings on the forehead of the tiger

Done   Internet

▲ *The tiger has always been prominent as a symbol in Asian cultures. In India, the species represents beauty, ferocity, and power. Children in China paint the symbol of the tiger in wine and mercury on their foreheads for good health.*

the tiger's fur. Ever since, the legend says, tigers have worn black stripes on their orange-gold coats.[5]

▶ An Endangered Species

Folktales aside, the tiger is surely not slow-witted. In real life, these powerful predators rule their wild domains much as lions rule the African plains. A full-grown tiger can take down prey as large as water buffalo and small elephants. Only human beings, armed with axes, plows, and rifles, have been able to turn the tiger into an endangered species.

The numbers tell the story. One hundred years ago, at least fifty thousand tigers lived in India. Another fifty thousand roamed habitats from Siberia to Indonesia. Today the total number of wild tigers is said to fall between 5,000 and 7,000.[6] Since the 1940s, the Bali, Caspian, and Javan subspecies have become extinct.

Before the practice was banned, trophy hunters shot thousands of tigers. Today the threat of extinction comes mainly from loss of habitat, as well as the demand for tiger skins and body parts for healing remedies. From whiskers to tail, every part of the tiger is used in folk medicine throughout Asia. Until the tiger becomes worth more alive than dead, its future is in serious jeopardy. Modern medicines made from plants, rather than tiger body parts, must be promoted and made readily available. Also, the protection of natural resources needs to be encouraged and aided. Such efforts are necessary to prevent humans from further intruding on the tiger's habitat. The first step, wildlife experts insist, is to understand how the big cat lives in the wild.

▲ If food is scarce, tigers will prey on large animals like these elephants, as well as small animals like monkeys and snakes.

An Awesome Predator

Kailash Sankhala has had a lifelong love affair with wildlife. In the 1970s, as the head of Project Tiger, Sankhala led the fight to save the Bengal tiger. He painted a word picture of this awesome predator:

> The [Bengal] Tiger is a creature of hypnotic power and fascination. A glimpse through green foliage of the sleek golden body gliding by like a phantom is an experience that no words can describe. . . . The more one sees of this beautiful beast the more one is charmed by its gorgeous color, the vivid pattern of the stripes on the glossy skin, the strength of the muscles, and the grace of the tiger's movements.[1]

Naturalists who study the tiger share Sankhala's sense of awe. Their

◀ *Tigers, classically orange-gold and black stripped, are majestic, sleek, and muscular. Natural-born predators, their strong jaws and explosive speed enable these animals to provide for themselves.*

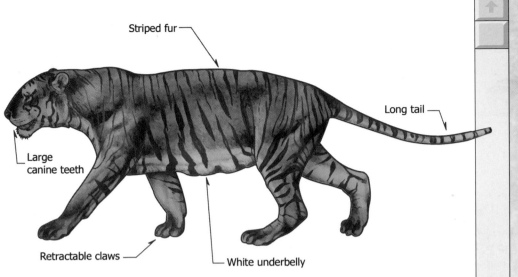

Striped fur

Long tail

Large canine teeth

Retractable claws

White underbelly

devoted—and often risky—work provides a detailed picture of the big cat's life cycle.

▶ What Makes a Tiger a Tiger?

The fossil record tells us that the tiger evolved in southern China. By modern times, tigers had spread across much of Asia. Today their habitats stretch from eastern Siberia in the north to the Caspian Sea in the west. In the south, tigers roam the forests of India and Indonesia.

In each region, the species adapted to local conditions. Life in cold northern forests created the largest of all tigers, the Siberian. A male Siberian tiger (*P. tigris altaica*) measures some thirteen feet (3.96 m) from its nose to the tip of its tail. Its extra thick coat helps it survive nights as cold as −49°F (−45°C). India's Bengal tiger (*P. tigris tigris*) is about two feet shorter. The Sumatran tiger (*P. tigris sumatrae*) is smaller still. Male Bengal tigers weigh about 400 pounds (181.4 kg). As in many species, the females are smaller than the males. Female Bengal tigers average eight feet in length and weigh some 300 pounds (136.1 kg).[2]

The Indochinese tiger (*P. tigris corbetti*) is smaller still. The females are usually less than nine feet (2.74 m) long, and weigh up to 287 pounds (130.2 kg).

The tiger's body is well equipped for stalking and killing. The strong, supple muscles power the explosive charge that brings a hunt to a successful end. Long, sharp canine teeth, strong jaw muscles, and retractable claws complete the tiger's weaponry. Keen eyes and ears make up for the lack of an acute sense of smell. Like all cats, the tiger has a rough, gritty tongue. The tongue is good for grooming—and for licking the meat off bones.

The tiger's classic orange-gold, black-striped coat blends almost invisibly into dry brush. It provides good camouflage in forests and grasslands. The stripes, naturalists believe, are really stretched-out spots. White patches are found around the eyes, cheeks, legs, and on the belly. Two bright white spots behind the ears are thought to help cubs follow their mother through tall grass.[3] White Bengal tigers are often bred for zoos and circus acts, but the mutation is rare in the wild. A *mutation* is a genetic change in an animal's inherited traits, such as the color of its coat—for example, white instead of orange-gold. Orange-gold is the dominant, or stronger, trait meaning that it occurs more often in nature.

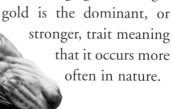

Most tigers are orange and black. White tigers are a result of a mutation of genes and are bred for circuses and zoos.

It is not known how often white tigers appear in the wild. In the last hundred years, only about a dozen white tigers have been seen in India. The white tiger collection in North American zoos traces its ancestry to Mohan, a single white male tiger. Mohan was captured in 1951 in central India. It did not take long for the maharajah—a king or prince of a large territory in India—who captured Mohan to figure out how to produce additional white tiger cubs. The only way was to breed Mohan with one of his own female cubs. Both the National Zoo in Washington, D.C., and the Cincinnati Zoo in Ohio can trace their white tiger line to Mohini, one of Mohan's "granddaughters."[4] This process of breeding related offspring is called inbreeding, which has been know to result in birth defects.

► Eating Like a Tiger

Meat is the mainstay of the tiger's diet—lots of meat. Tigers eat forty to fifty hoofed mammals a year. A female Bengal tiger needs an average of thirteen pounds (5.89 kg) of meat a day, which averages 2 to 3 percent of a tiger's body weight. If the female is raising cubs, that requirement jumps to eighteen pounds a day (8.16 kilograms). Over a year, that translates into forty to seventy kills. Since most tigers succeed in bringing down their prey only one time in ten, hunting is a full-time job. In dense jungles, the ratio may fall to one kill in twenty tries. If hunting is poor, tigers fill up on edible plants such as grass, berries, and sugar cane.[5]

Driven by their fierce appetites, tigers zero in on larger animals. One favorite is the wild ox, known as the gaur. A half-ton gaur will feed a tiger and her cubs for a week or more. Although the flesh starts to decay in a few days, tigers do not mind. They feed on a carcass until only a few scraps of bone and hide are left. If large hoofed

▲ Large hoofed mammals, such as this spotted deer, are the tigers favorite meal.

animals are scarce, tigers hunt fish, monkeys, porcupines, peacocks, and snakes—even termites.

Each year a few tigers become man-eaters. Once they lose their fear of humans, the big cats can be deadly. The champion killer was India's Champawat tigress. During a four-year killing spree from 1907 to 1911, this female tiger killed 236 people.[6] In 1937, hunter and conservationist Jim Corbett tracked down and finally killed the Champawat tigress, but not before she had killed 436 people. Today, even with far fewer tigers, the problem persists. In the first three months of 2002, tigers killed twenty-two people in Bangladesh.

It is uncertain why tigers become man-eaters. Some think that the tiger may have dental problems, such as broken or lost teeth, or injuries that keep them from hunting their natural prey. Humans are easier to kill than deer and other wildlife, so when a tiger is injured, it must kill what it can to survive. Wildlife experts also blame poachers for making tigers become man-eaters. Poachers are people who hunt tigers for their skins and body parts. The heavy poaching, some experts say, teaches tigers to view humans as enemies.[7]

▶ A Solitary Life Cycle

Unlike the lion, the tiger is a solitary creature. A mature male Bengal tiger rules a territory as large as forty square miles (64.37 sq. km.). As the male patrols his range, he marks his boundaries with a spray of urine and scent. The tiger also claws deep gouges in tree trunks. As a final warning, the male lets loose a roar that can be heard three miles away. For mating purposes, the male allows two to seven females to occupy smaller ranges within his realm. The male largely ignores this harem (group of females) until one of the females signals that she is ready to mate.

Scent marks and earthshaking roars bring the pair together. Courtship is a rough, noisy process. The tigers growl, circle, bite, and wrestle. At times they rear up on their hind legs and paw at each other like boxers. The pair mates many times, and may take time out to hunt together. After two or three days, each tiger goes its own way.

The tigress carries her unborn cubs for 93 to 111 days. As the time to give birth nears, the pregnant tiger beds down in a rocky crevice or under a fallen log. There the female produces a litter of two to seven two-pound (.91 kg) cubs. In larger litters, the weaker cubs often die in the first few days. From the moment of birth, the tigress guards the blind and helpless cubs with a savage fury.

▲ In the past, the biggest threats to tiger cubs were injury or disease.
Now it is human beings who cause the loss of the tigers' habitat and
hunt the species for its different parts.

At the first sign of threat, the new mother moves the cubs
to a new den. No one is allowed close, not even the
cubs' father.

For the first two months, the tigress leaves the den
only to hunt. At about eight weeks of age, the cubs will
start eating meat. However, they will not wean themselves
from their mother until about three to six months of age.
As the cubs grow larger, the female allows them to tag
along on hunts. When the female makes a kill, she calls the
cubs to share the bounty. Unlike a lioness, the tigress
allows the cubs to eat first. By six months, the growing,

playful cubs are ready to start survival lessons. The mother may begin by disabling a deer. Then she calls the cubs to finish the kill. Six months later, the cubs graduate to stalking their own game. Unlike most cats, tigers love to swim. If a cub holds back during swimming lessons, the tigress is likely to drop it into the water.[8] Being a good swimmer can be an advantage for a tiger. Tigers are ambush hunters. Often a tiger will wait in the tall grass along a river or lake for deer and other animals to come get a drink.

Two-year-olds range farther and farther away. The tigress, in turn, is ready to mate again. After she gives birth, she chases off the grown cubs if they try to visit the new litter. Female cubs often settle near their mothers, who shift their own ranges to make room. A male cub faces a sterner test. Instinct drives him to try to take over an older male's territory. Most male cubs fail, and some die in the attempt. By the time the young male is four, he may be strong and clever enough to win this crucial battle.[9]

In a typical litter, half the cubs perish before their second birthday. Intruding older males kill some. Others drown in floods or die from injuries or disease. All too often, cubs and adults alike fall victim to the greatest threat of all—human beings.

Chapter 3

Threats to the Tiger's Survival

A stroll through a noisy, crowded Chinese street market reveals stalls piled high with food, tools, clothing, and toys. Down some side street there are tables stocked with traditional Chinese medicines.

There is a medicine for every ailment. Many of the pills and salves are made from herbs, roots, and tree bark.

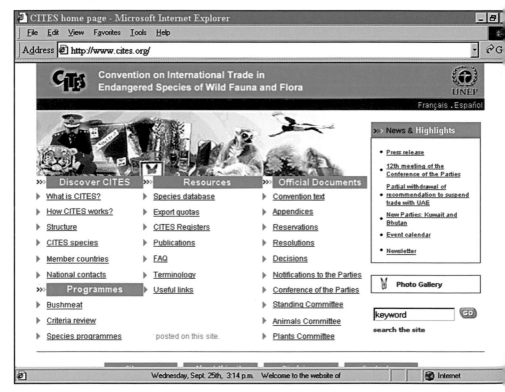

▲ The Convention on International Trade in Endangered Species of Wild Fauna and Flora has been adopted by a total of 160 countries around the world since it entered into force on July 1, 1975. No species protected by CITES has become extinct as a result of trade.

Others are made from animals—dogs, goats, rhino, sheep, and tigers. Powdered tiger bone is considered a remedy for arthritis. A single pill costs about $2.50. Seven hundred fifty-two dollars will fetch a tiger paw.[1] Tiger brain is used to treat acne. In ancient China, tiger whiskers were used to poison enemies. Today they are used to treat toothaches.

The sale of tiger parts outrages conservationists. Because tigers are protected by law, the market is mostly underground. Even so, South Korea imports a thousand pounds of tiger bones each year. At least fifty tigers must die to supply all those bones. High profits help drive the trade. A poacher can earn $8,000 by selling the pelt, body parts, and bones to a dealer. Processed and sold part by part, a dead tiger can generate profits of up to $750,000.[2]

The people who use tiger medications are certain they work. "We're not trying to kill tigers," says folk medicine expert David Choy. "We're trying to save human lives. The laws . . . are good for tigers but not for people."[3] Choy's claims fill animal lovers with dread—and poaching is not the only threat to tigers.

Natural Perils

For all their size and power, tigers do succumb to natural causes. Some big cats die of wounds and broken bones. They suffer the injuries in fights with rivals, in falls, and while hunting. Even a minor injury can be fatal. A cub that tackles a porcupine is likely to wind up with a quill stuck in its lip. If the wound becomes infected, the cub will weaken and die. Tigers also drown in floods and perish in forest fires. Disease can play a role as well. Canine distemper, for example, killed hundreds of Tanzania's lions in 1994. A similar outbreak could wipe out a wild tiger population.[4]

Today's tigers also face danger from a less visible threat. Suppose that a park's population has dwindled to forty tigers. As a rule, only sixteen or so will produce cubs. Genetic diversity is lost as fathers mate with daughters and mothers mate with sons. In time, fewer cubs will be born. Those that do survive are likely to be less successful as adults, because inbreeding weakens a species. Geneticist Steve O'Brien explains, "Variation is good, because . . . it provides flexibility of the species to adapt to changes."[5] Zoos that breed tigers do what they can to promote genetic diversity. When choosing a mating pair, breeders try to match a female with a male from a different regions.

▶ Loss of Habitat

At current growth rates, the human population of Southeast Asia doubles every thirty-seven years.[6] Feeding and clothing all those people puts a severe strain on natural resources. Animal prey and predators vanish as villagers scour the countryside for game. Naturalist George Schaller once asked some villagers in Laos if there were Indochinese tigers nearby. He knew that the big cats once were common in the region. "Yes, one came by here a year ago," they told him.[7]

A typical battle in the war for habitat took place on a reserve in India in the early 1990s. The conflict began with a long drought. As their fields shriveled, villagers drove their livestock into the reserve to graze. The herds soon overgrazed the grasslands, leaving the park's deer, wild boar, and gazelles little to eat. Looking for prey, the local tigers turned to the villagers' cattle, water buffalo, and goats. To protect their animals, the herders struck back with guns, traps, and poison. Rather than stop the villagers, the reserve's guards stepped aside and allowed what amounted to an organized slaughter of tigers.[8]

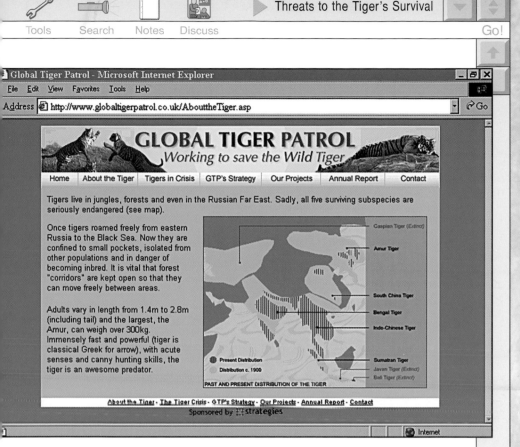

Global Tiger Patrol - Microsoft Internet Explorer

File Edit View Favorites Tools Help

Address http://www.globaltigerpatrol.co.uk/AbouttheTiger.asp

GLOBAL TIGER PATROL
Working to save the Wild Tiger

Home | About the Tiger | Tigers in Crisis | GTP's Strategy | Our Projects | Annual Report | Contact

Tigers live in jungles, forests and even in the Russian Far East. Sadly, all five surviving subspecies are seriously endangered (see map).

Once tigers roamed freely from eastern Russia to the Black Sea. Now they are confined to small pockets, isolated from other populations and in danger of becoming inbred. It is vital that forest "corridors" are kept open so that they can move freely between areas.

Adults vary in length from 1.4m to 2.8m (including tail) and the largest, the Amur, can weigh over 300kg. Immensely fast and powerful (tiger is classical Greek for arrow), with acute senses and canny hunting skills, the tiger is an awesome predator.

Caspian Tiger (Extinct)
Amur Tiger
South China Tiger
Bengal Tiger
Indo-Chinese Tiger
Sumatran Tiger
Javan Tiger (Extinct)
Bali Tiger (Extinct)

Present Distribution
Distribution c. 1900

PAST AND PRESENT DISTRIBUTION OF THE TIGER

About the Tiger · The Tiger Crisis · GTP's Strategy · Our Projects · Annual Report · Contact
Sponsored by :: strategies

Internet

▲ At one time, tigers roamed freely in Asia. Now the five surviving subspecies are isolated in small areas.

Since 1900, tiger habitats—and tiger populations—have been reduced by about 95 percent.[9] All across Asia, prime forest has been turned into barren wasteland. The culprits include heavy logging, overgrazing, dam building, and erosion. Adding to the damage, cattle sometimes infect wild deer herds with viral diseases. As their prey disappears, tigers move elsewhere—or vanish.

▷ The Ultimate Predator

Alone and unarmed, a human is no match for a tiger. Give the human a high-powered rifle, a vial of poison, or a steel trap, and the tiger is still dangerous, but now the odds

favor the human. If the human is a skilled poacher, there is a good chance the tiger will be killed. If a culture values wildlife less than the animal's value in the marketplace, the killing will go on until there are no more tigers.

The struggle between man and tiger was not always so uneven. A hundred years ago, tigers killed hundreds of people each year. To protect villagers, Indian rulers organized tiger-hunting expeditions. When the British came to India, army officers took up the challenge. Mounted on elephants or perched high in the trees, they shot tigers by the thousands. During a four-year span in the 1850s, one sharpshooter killed ninety-three tigers. Only when the tiger population fell to alarmingly low numbers in the

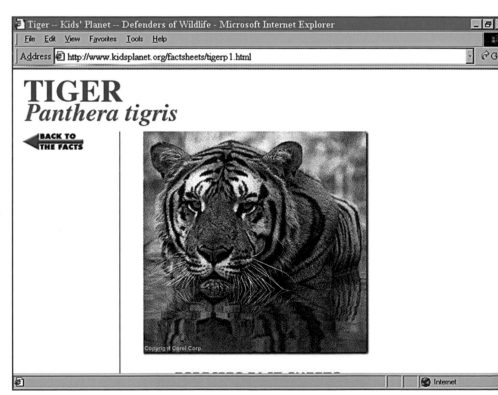

▲ Tigers differ from most cats in that they like the water.

1960s did the government ban hunting. To protect the surviving tigers, parks and reserves were set aside.[10]

The killing reached new heights in China after World War II. Communist leader Mao Tse-tung needed land for new farms, factories, and villages. To clear the way, Mao declared that tigers were an "enemy of the People." The slaughter that followed almost wiped out the Chinese tiger (*P. tigris amoyensis*) and put many tiger parts on the market. As a side effect, with tiger bone and parts plentiful, the demand for tiger-medicines shot up. When the supply of Chinese tiger parts ran low, high prices inspired an upsurge in poaching in India and Sumatra.[11] Only in recent years have the Chinese taken steps to save their few remaining tigers.

Today illegal hunting and poaching endanger all wild tigers. Naturalists explain that for every ten tigers killed, another fifteen are likely to die. If a villager poisons a nursing mother, her young cubs are unlikely to survive. Next, poachers might kill the old male who ruled the forty-square-mile realm. His death opens the way for younger males to compete for his title. The winner will try to kill the old ruler's male cubs so he can father his own litters.[12]

Threatened from all sides, the tiger is truly an endangered species. The one-sided battle might have been lost long ago, except for a worldwide save-the-tiger campaign.

Chapter 4

Save the Tiger!

The light began to dawn in the late 1960s. Unless something was done, and done quickly, the tiger would soon be extinct. Critics, from barefoot villagers to penny-pinching government officials, said the price was too high. "Tigers eat people," they grumbled. "Who needs them?"

▶ Operation Tiger Kicks Off

The news that tigers are endangered was slow in catching the world's notice. At last, in 1972, the World Wildlife

▲ *People from all over the world are coming together to save the tiger. India has twenty-five parks and wildlife reserves dedicated to protecting these animals.*

Fund (WWF) launched a save-the-tiger campaign. Money poured in for Operation Tiger as the public awoke to the threat. Soon women who wore tiger fur coats were being booed as they walked down the street.[1] Countries large and small agreed to stop importing and exporting endangered species.

India, home of the Bengal tiger, kicked off Project Tiger in 1973. Prime Minister Indira Gandhi signed the law that set up the country's first wildlife reserve, called Bandipur National Park. Ranthambhore National Park and other reserves followed. Next came the hard, day-to-day work. Roads had to be built, and villagers had to be moved to new homes. Guards enforced new rules that outlawed hunting and logging. Fines were handed out to farmers who let their herds graze in the reserves. By 1998, India could point with pride to twenty-five parks and reserves. As other Asian countries set up their own reserves, tigers staged a modest comeback.

▶ Adding the Rule of Law

The fight to save the tiger extends far beyond Asia. Many governments have been writing laws that add muscle to the enforcement movement. One major victory came in 1973. With United Nations backing, more than 120 countries signed the CITES (pronounced SIGH-tees) treaty. CITES stands for the Convention on International Trade in Endangered Species of Wild Fauna and Flora. The agreement puts strict controls on the sale of endangered plants and animals. Nations that violate the rules can be cut off from markets or denied loans.

Americans have played a key role in defending the tiger. Congress helped by passing the Endangered Species Act in 1967. The act provides fines of $12,000 and

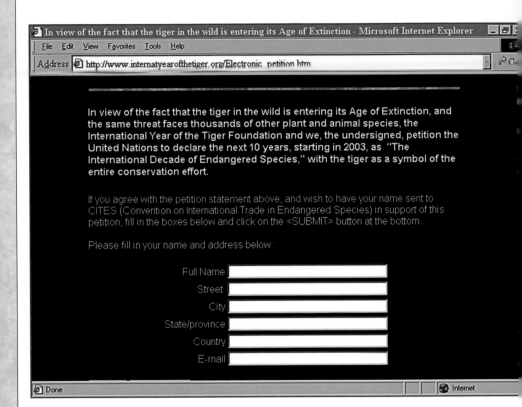

In view of the fact that the tiger in the wild is entering its Age of Extinction - Microsoft Internet Explorer

File   Edit   View   Favorites   Tools   Help

Address ❤ http://www.internatyearofthetiger.org/Electronic_petition.htm

In view of the fact that the tiger in the wild is entering its Age of Extinction, and the same threat faces thousands of other plant and animal species, the International Year of the Tiger Foundation and we, the undersigned, petition the United Nations to declare the next 10 years, starting in 2003, as "The International Decade of Endangered Species," with the tiger as a symbol of the entire conservation effort.

If you agree with the petition statement above, and wish to have your name sent to CITES (Convention on International Trade in Endangered Species) in support of this petition, fill in the boxes below and click on the <SUBMIT> button at the bottom.

Please fill in your name and address below:

Full Name
Street
City
State/province
Country
E-mail

Done   Internet

▲ *You may sign petitions online to save the tiger or print one to distribute amongst your friends and family. These are made available by groups such as the International Year of the Tiger Foundation.*

six-month jail terms for anyone who kills or sells an endangered plant or animal.[2] In 1994, the Rhinoceros and Tiger Conservation Act made the act easier to enforce. The new law also opened the door to using tax dollars for rhino and tiger conservation. The business world joined in as Exxon Oil kicked off a fund-raising drive. (Exxon often uses an image of a tiger in their advertisements.) Caught up in the campaign to save the tigers, Americans whipped out their checkbooks. Tiger conservation groups, fueled by the influx of cash, redoubled their efforts.

Wildlife experts agree that passing laws and giving money are helpful first steps. The harder work, they say, must be done on the ground. Setting up tiger reserves is a good step—but the reserves must support a healthy prey population. Antipoaching laws are good—but only if they are enforced. Banning livestock from the forest is good—but only if villagers are given better ways to feed their herds. In short, protecting the tiger needs a balanced, long-term commitment.

Ranthambhore: A Case Study

Ranthambhore National Park in north-central India is a well-known tiger reserve. The park sprawls across 150-square miles of upland forests and grasslands.[3] Peacocks call from crumbling hilltop forts that once guarded a local ruler's game preserve. Spotted deer and wild boar drink at the park's three lakes. A sign at the railway station welcomes visitors to the "City of Tigers."

Project Tiger reached Ranthambhore in 1973. Game warden Fateh Singh saw that only a handful of tigers still roamed the park. Strong measures were needed. Using force when persuasion failed, Singh moved entire villages out of the park. Next, his guards kept local herdsmen from grazing their livestock in the park. This tough approach upset the local people. Denied access to the forest, they saw an age-old way of life vanishing.

Indian conservationist Valmik Thapar saw the problem clearly. "It is no longer enough to police the tiger forests of the world," he writes. "Legislation to protect the forests has to be supported by the people who live in and around them. Only if this happens do the forest and its wildlife have a chance of surviving."[4] To enlist that support, Thapar formed the Ranthambhore Foundation. The foundation's experts

Humans have become the tigers' number one threat.

introduced the villagers to new methods of conserving water and soil. They encouraged farmers to plant trees and raise new crops. Some of the crops fed village families. Others crops produced fuel for cook fires and fodder to feed domestic animals.[5]

For a time, the two-pronged approach seemed to pay off. In the mid-1980s, a report noted that as many as forty tigers were living in the park. Then nature took a hand. A seven-year drought drove herdsmen into the park in search of grass for their livestock. This time, Fateh Singh was not there to turn them back. His no-nonsense methods had cost him his job. To make matters worse, the poachers returned. By the late 1990s, the number of tigers in the park had dwindled to twelve. Singh worried that the number might be as low as eight.[6]

As writer Peter Matthiessen notes, "Under the noses of sixty forest guards, the missing animals had been shot and poisoned so rapidly . . . that they were gone before the park authorities noticed."[7] Fateh Singh, who still lives near Ranthambhore, worries that his beloved tigers will soon be gone. Asked what will happen to the City of Tigers if the big cats vanish from the park, he sighed. "Maybe," he said, "they can call it the City of Peacocks."[8]

A Cloudy Future

During a visit to a Buddhist temple in Hong Kong, a small boy caught the eye of journalist Andrew Lam. The boy looked puzzled as he traced a carving of dragons and tigers with his fingers.

"Mama," he asked, "does the tiger really exist, or is it just like the dragon?"

His mother shrugged. "It is still real, but not for very long. Soon it will be like the dragon."[1]

Lam worries that the mother may have spoken the truth. The countdown to extinction clock is still ticking. As wildlife expert John Seidensticker puts it, "Tigers won't ultimately be safe until they're worth more alive than dead."[2]

What Do the Numbers Say?

At first glance, the estimate that 5,000 to 7,000 tigers survive in the wild may sound hopeful. Several troubling facts hint at a less positive future. At

At one time, 100,000 tigers roamed Asia. This has now been reduced to only 5,000 to 7,000 tigers.

least 100,000 tigers once roamed freely in Asia. In 1931, India was home to 131 million people. By 1999, the population had raced well past the 1 billion mark. The rising tide of people competes with wildlife for space, food, and fuel. Solitary, free-ranging tigers are hard to count. Wildlife experts worry. They fear that park officials (whose jobs may depend on keeping tigers safe) are reporting "ghost" tigers, and lying about the total number.[3] Even the widely used bottom-line figure of five thousand wild tigers may be too high.

Once again, the Ranthambhore reserve makes the case. Today the park supports fewer tigers than it did in the dark days of the 1960s. The evidence of the falloff is not hard to find. On an evening visit, a guest spots hundreds of wild boar and at least eighty piglets feeding near a lake. Fateh Singh, the former game warden, agrees that it is a lovely sight—but a bad sign. "These are easy meals for tigers," he says. "Too many piglets are an indicator that predation is nearing zero."[4]

▶ Can Captive Tigers Save the Day?

The big cats that are so elusive in the wild are easy to find in cages. One estimate puts the number of captive tigers as high as fifteen thousand or more. Caged tigers are common in zoos, safari parks, carnivals, and sanctuaries. Many sanctuaries have rescued tigers from owners who could not handle it when their cute little cubs grew up to be scary, 400-pound (181.44 kg) adults.[5]

Some people look at captive cubs and say, "Raise the cubs to adulthood. Then return them to the wild!" If the cure were that simple, Asia's reserves would be filled with tigers. As zoologist Valmik Thapar points out, captive tigers do not learn how to hunt. Set free in the wild, they

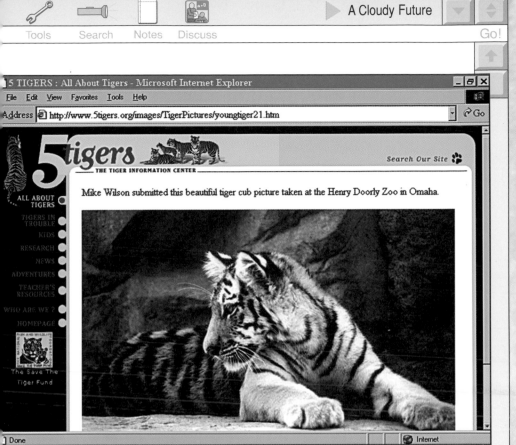

5 TIGERS : All About Tigers - Microsoft Internet Explorer

File   Edit   View   Favorites   Tools   Help

Address http://www.5tigers.org/images/TigerPictures/youngtiger21.htm

5tigers
THE TIGER INFORMATION CENTER

Search Our Site

ALL ABOUT TIGERS
TIGERS IN TROUBLE
KIDS
RESEARCH
NEWS
ADVENTURES
TEACHER'S RESOURCES
WHO ARE WE ?
HOMEPAGE

The Save The Tiger Fund

Mike Wilson submitted this beautiful tiger cub picture taken at the Henry Doorly Zoo in Omaha.

Done   Internet

▲ Once tigers live in captivity, they may never be released into the wild.

lack the skills needed to bring down wild prey. Driven by hunger, they may turn to feeding on domestic cattle—or human beings.[6]

Sarah Christie, of the London Zoo, argues that the problem can be solved. She suggests the following plan: Put a pair of captive tigers in a large enclosure in good tiger country. Feed them with live animals. Then when cubs are born, they will learn to stalk and kill their prey. Eighteen months later, free the half-grown cubs. With any luck they will migrate to new ranges and succeed as wild adults.[7] Christie may be right, but no one knows for sure.

		STOP					
Back	Forward	Stop	Review	Home	Explore	Favorites	History

Even in cages, captive tigers aid their own cause. A public that learns to admire the tiger's grace and beauty is more likely to pitch in to help save it. Zoos also work to safeguard genetic diversity. Mating females with males from different bloodlines produces active, healthy cubs. These cubs, in turn, will help carry on the species. One organization, The Tiger Missing Link Foundation, of Tyler, Texas, is working to identify all the subspecies that are in captivity in the United States. Tigers whose parents were both of the same subspecies, are pure bred, and vital to the success of conservation programs.

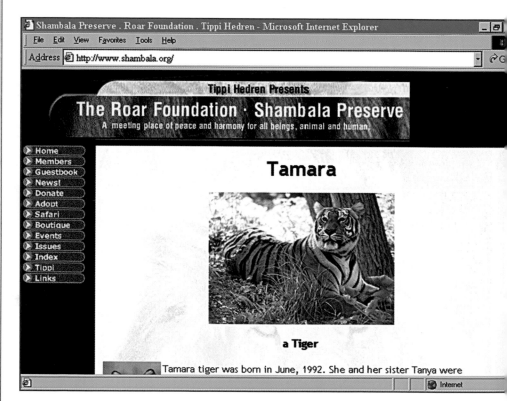

Tamara was rescued from a man selling tiger cubs out of his station wagon at a mall in Orange County, California. She now lives with almost seventy other animals at the Shambala Preserve on the edge of the Mohave Desert in California.

Darker chapters in the story of captive tigers are played out in secret. In 1992, for example, "tiger farming" in Taiwan was exposed in a shocking video. The bootlegged film opened with shots of a breeding farm where tigers were raised in cages. Further footage proved that the "tiger farmers" were raising the animals to be butchered. The parts then were sold for high prices in Asian markets.[8]

All Is Not Lost

In the end, the fight to save the tiger hinges on a few basic facts. There are fourteen Asian countries where tigers live in the wild. In some of these countries, it is taken for granted that the forests will always exist. As more humans are born there, villagers put greater stress on wild habitats. Saving the wild tiger, therefore, means safeguarding wildlife reserves. As zoologist Alan Rabinowitz puts it, "There can be no chipping away at the edges, no human settlements . . . no commercial exploitation." The reality, he says, is that "forest guards must be better paid . . . and better trained and better armed than the poachers. Otherwise the battle is lost from the beginning."[9]

Reforming the folk medicine market, experts say, will further cut poaching. Roots and herbs can replace the tiger parts used to treat illnesses. Insomniacs need not depend on tiger claw broth for relief. Coptis root and wild jujube seed could work just as well. Cork tree bark can replace powdered tiger bone to treat joint pain. A toothache can be relieved with ginseng instead of tiger whiskers.[10] As more and more people switch to plant remedies, the market for tiger parts will shrink.

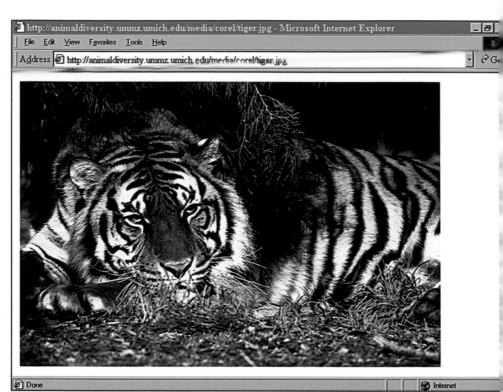

http://animaldiversity.ummz.umich.edu/media/corel/tiger.jpg - Microsoft Internet Explorer

File Edit View Favorites Tools Help

Address http://animaldiversity.ummz.umich.edu/media/corel/tiger.jpg

Done   Internet

▲ In folk medicine, some parts of the tiger are used as treatment for illnesses. Help save the tiger by reporting the sale of tiger products to your local police.

▶ What Can You Do?

Action film star Jackie Chan is a spokesman for ACAP, the Asian Conservation Awareness Programme. In his talks, Chan tells audiences that everyone must help the tiger fight for survival. No matter where you live, you can help save the tiger and other endangered species. Share what you have learned about tigers. Get out the word about endangered species. You can start with your family and friends. Tell them not to buy tiger products.

Alert police if you see tiger products on sale. Warn buyers and sellers alike that they are risking heavy fines, or even jail. Also, support campaigns to raise money for conservation efforts such as Project Tiger. Conservation groups raise money worldwide and work with local officials to help save endangered species. Finally, write or e-mail your elected officials. Ask them to do more to protect the tiger and other endangered species.[11]

All across the globe, people of goodwill are joining hands to save the greatest of all predators. Will their efforts pay off? Tiger lovers admit that the future is clouded. Human populations are growing at an alarming rate. People must have places to live, food to eat, and jobs to support them. Old customs, such as using tiger parts for medicines and tiger pelts for rugs, are difficult for people to stop doing. In the midst of the tumult, tigers require space and solitude. If humans cannot guarantee those basic needs, the wild tiger may well be doomed.

The Endangered and Threatened Wildlife List

This series is based on the Endangered and Threatened Wildlife list compiled by the U.S. Fish and Wildlife Service (USFWS). Each book explores an endangered or threatened animal, tells why it has become endangered or threatened, and explains the efforts being made to restore the species' population.

The United States Fish and Wildlife Service, in the Department of the Interior, and the National Marine Fisheries Service, in the Department of Commerce, share responsibility for administration of the Endangered Species Act.

In 1973, Congress took the farsighted step of creating the Endangered Species Act, widely regarded as the world's strongest and most effective wildlife conservation law. It set an ambitious goal: to reverse the alarming trend of human-caused extinction that threatened the ecosystems we all share.

The complete list of Endangered and Threatened Wildlife and Plants can be found at
http://endangered.fws.gov/wildlife.html#Species

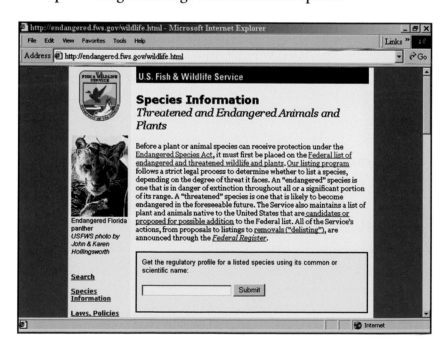

Chapter Notes

Chapter 1. *Panthera tigris*

1. "The Evolution of the Felids," *Forever Tigers*, n.d., <http://www.forevertigers.com/evolution.htm> (Oct. 23, 2002).

2. Ibid.

3. Peter Matthiessen, *Tigers in the Snow* (San Diego, Calif.: Lucent Books, 1999), p. 14.

4. Quoted in Michael Nichols and Geoffrey C. Ward, *The Year of the Tiger* (Washington, D.C.: National Geographic Society, 1998), p. 2.

5. Alan Rabinowitz, *Chasing the Dragon's Tail: The Struggle to Save Thailand's Wild Cats* (New York: Anchor Books, 1991), pp. 194–195.

6. "Populations," *Tigers in the Wild*, n.d., <http://www.panda.org/resources/publications/specics/tiger99/tiger_glance.html> (May 8, 2002).

Chapter 2. An Awesome Predator

1. Kailash Sankhala, *Tiger! The Story of the Indian Tiger* (New York: Simon & Schuster, 1977), p. 24.

2. Patricia A. Michaels, "Endangered Species: Tigers," *Tigers Fact Sheet*, 2001, <http://environment.about.com/library/weekly/bles4a.htm> (May 8, 2002).

3. K. Ullas Karanth, *The Way of the Tiger: Natural History and Conservation of the Endangered Big Cat* (Stillwater, Minn.: Voyageur Press, 2001), p. 48.

4. Ronald L. Tilson, "White Tigers," *5 Tigers: The Tiger Information Center*, n.d., <http://www.5tigers.org/> (Oct. 7, 2002).

5. Michael Nichols and Geoffrey C. Ward, *The Year of the Tiger* (Washington, D.C.: National Geographic Society, 1998), p. 32.

6. Karanth, p. 63.

7. "Tiger Deaths Soar in Bangladesh," *5 Tigers: the Tiger Information Center,* April 3, 2002, <http://www.5tigers.org/news/2002/April/02_4_3w1.htm> (April 8, 2002).

8. Sankhala, pp. 76–77.

9. Karanth, p. 72.

Chapter 3. Threats to the Tiger's Survival

1. Michael Dorgan, "Tigers in Trouble: Sale of Parts, Even Fakes, Hastening Extinction," *Knight Ridder Newspapers,* March 9, 2001, <http://groups.google.com/groups?q=tigers+endangered&start=10&hl=en&lr=&selm=9918nu01eed%40drn.newsguy.com&rnum=18> (April 16, 2002).

2. Peter Matthiessen, *Tigers in the Snow* (San Diego, Calif.: Lucent Books, 1999), p. 114.

3. Cory J. Meacham, *How the Tiger Lost Its Stripes: an Exploration into the Endangerment of a Species* (New York: Harcourt Brace & Co., 1997), p. 147.

4. "Impact of Catastrophes," *Tigers in the Wild,* n.d., <http://www.panda.org/resources/publications/species/tiger99/catastrophe.html> (May 8, 2002).

5. Meacham, p. 8.

6. "Poaching and Habitat Loss," *Tigers in the Wild,* n.d., <http://www.panda.org/resources/publications/species/tiger99/poaching.html> (May 8, 2002).

7. Michael Nichols and Geoffrey C. Ward, *The Year of the Tiger* (Washington, D.C.: National Geographic Society, 1998), p. 33.

8. Matthiessen, p. 81.

9. "About the Crisis," *Endangered Earth: Tigers in Crisis,* n.d., <http://www.tigersincrisis.com/about_page6.htm> (February 5, 2002).

10. Kailash Sankhala, *Tiger! The Story of the Indian Tiger* (New York: Simon & Schuster, 1977), p. 90.

11. "Plight of the Tiger," *Forever Tigers,* n.d., <http://www.forevertigers.com/plight.htm> (April 22, 2002).

12. Ibid.

Chapter 4. Save the Tiger!

1. Simon Barnes, *Tiger!* (New York: St. Martin's Press, 1994), p. 128.

2. "Endangered Species Medicine," *Tigers in the Wild,* n.d., <http://www.panda.org/resources/publications/species/tiger99/end_species_medicine.html> (May 8, 2002).

3. Quoted in Michael Nichols and Geoffrey C. Ward, *The Year of the Tiger* (Washington, D.C.: National Geographic Society, 1998), p. 44.

4. Valmik Thapar, *The Tiger's Destiny* (London: Kyle Cathie Ltd., Publishers, 1992), p. 168.

5. Peter Matthiessen, *Tigers in the Snow* (San Diego, Calif.: Lucent Books, 1999), pp. 80–81.

6. Stanley Breeden and Belinda Wright, *Through the Tiger's Eyes: a Chronicle of India's Wildlife,* (Berkeley, Calif.: Ten Speed Press, 1996), p. 153.

7. Matthiessen, p. 81.

8. Michael Nichols and Geoffrey C. Ward, *The Year of the Tiger* (Washington, D.C.: National Geographic Society, 1998), p. 29.

Chapter 5. A Cloudy Future

1. Andrew Lam, "Drinking Tiger Soup," *Forever Tigers,* 1996, <http://www.forevertigers.com/tigersoup.htm> (April 22, 2002).

2. Quoted in Michael Nichols and Geoffrey C. Ward, *The Year of the Tiger* (Washington, D.C.: National Geographic Society, 1998), p. 45.

3. Simon Barnes, *Tiger!* (New York: St. Martin's Press, 1994), p. 109.

4. Nichols, p. 28.

5. Ibid., pp. 84–87.

6. Cory J. Meacham, *How the Tiger Lost Its Stripes: an Exploration into the Endangerment of a Species* (New York: Harcourt Brace & Co., 1997), pp. 24–25.

7. Ibid., pp. 26–27.

8. Ibid., pp. 98–99.

9. Alan Rabinowitz, *Chasing the Dragon's Tail: the Struggle to Save Thailand's Wild Cats* (New York: Anchor Books, 1991), pp. 226–227.

10. "Traditional Chinese Medicine: Alternatives to Tiger Parts in Medicine," *Tigers in Crisis,* n.d., <http://www.tigersincrisis.com/solutions_2.htm> (April 8, 2002).

11. "What You Can Do," *Tigers in Summary,* n.d., <http://acapworldwide.com/tiger1.htm> (April 25, 2002).

Further Reading

Barnes, Simon. *Tiger!* New York: St. Martin's Press, 1994.

Breeden, Stanley and Belinda Wright. *Through the Tiger's Eyes: a Chronicle of India's Wildlife.* Berkeley, Calif.: Ten Speed Press, 1996.

Hornocker, Maurice, ed. *Track of the Tiger: Legend and Lore of the Great Cat.* San Francisco, Calif.: Sierra Club Books, 1997.

Ives, Richard. *Of Tigers and Men: Entering the Age of Extinction.* New York: Doubleday, 1996.

Karanth, K. Ullas. *The Way of the Tiger: Natural History and Conservation of the Endangered Big Cat.* Stillwater, Minn.: Voyageur Press, 2001.

Matthiessen, Peter. *Tigers in the Snow.* New York: North Point Press/Farrar, Strauss & Giroux, 2000.

Meacham, Cory J. *How the Tiger Lost Its Stripes: an Exploration into the Endangerment of a Species.* New York: Harcourt Brace & Co., 1997.

Nichols, Michael and Geoffrey C. Ward. *The Year of the Tiger.* Washington, D.C.: National Geographic Society, 1998.

Rabinowitz, Alan. *Chasing the Dragon's Tail: the Struggle to Save Thailand's Wild Cats.* New York: Doubleday, 1991.

Sankhala, Kailash. *Tiger! The Story of the Indian Tiger.* New York: Simon and Schuster, 1977.

Seidensticker, John, Sarah Christie and Peter Jackson. *Riding the Tiger: Tiger Conservation in Human-dominated Landscapes.* The Zoological Society of London. Cambridge: Cambridge University Press, 1999.

Singh, Arjan. *Tiger Haven.* New York: Harper & Row, Publishers, 1973.

Thapar, Valmik. *The Tiger's Destiny.* London: Kyle Cathie Ltd., Publishers, 1992.